TOUCHDOWN THE STORY OF THE CORNELL BEAR

John H. Foote

Tradition should be based on facts rather than be confused by wandering minstrels. Bear with me and I will set the matter straight for posterity.

S.E. (Booty) Hunkin '16
Manager, 1915 Cornell University
National Championship
Football Team
From a Letter to the Editor,
Cornell Alumni News
January 1966 issue

It is a pity that some one has not collected and set down these stories;properly arranged they would constitute a significant mythology, a Cornell epic which, whether literally true or only characteristic, would convey far better than official records in deans' offices the real significance of this institution. Some of these stories I have heard, and for their illustrative value will venture to recall a few of them. Like Herodotus, I give them as they were related to me without vouching for their truth, and like Herodotus, I hope no god or hero will take offense at what I say.

Address by Carl Becker,
"The Cornell Tradition:
Freedom and Responsibility"
April 27, 1940

For Kristen
and the university we love.

Cover photograh: Touchdown with the 1915 Big Red team in Atlantic City, New Jersey, November 1915.

Inside cover photographs: The stone bears flanking the fireplace in Willard Straight Hall's International Lounge.
Photo by Robert Barker.
Collection of the author.

Frontispiece: Touchdown III demonstrating on behalf of professors.

Printed in USA

ISBN: 978-1-5017-2653-8

Contents

I met the Cornell bear for the first time in Hamilton,
New York on an Indian summer day in September 1973.
The Big Red football team was playing Colgate, and at
halftime a group of Colgate students streamed out of
the stands and began to chase the Cornell mascot—
a student dressed in a faux fur bear suit that was
moth-eaten and odiferous, with an over-sized head in
which one eye was enlarged to allow the passage of a
12-ounce beer can.

Under the best of circumstances, it was difficult for the
wearer of this get-up to see what was going on. In the
case of the 1973 bear, the wearer was actually legally
blind, making it all but impossible for him to see the
mob coming across the field. He heard, however, the
Cornell cheerleaders, myself included, yelling that the
Colgate students were about to converge, and he took
off running, straight into the goalpost, knocking himself out cold.

Seeing the bear lying inert in the end zone, we ran over
and pulled off his head, and made his acquaintance
when he came to. This was the beginning of a wonderful
three months of road trips, Moosemilk, and hijinks. To
this day, the fellow who was the Cornell bear in the fall
of 1973 remains an unforgettable character and a good
friend, and is probably the reason why the topic of this
book is of particular interest to me.

Most Cornellians today believe that a bear has been the mascot of the Big Red athletic teams and a symbol of Cornell since the University's earliest days. Certainly a bear has become a familiar image on campus, striking poses of fierce determination, playfulness, or a college student hanging out with a mug in hand. Make-believe bears like my friend stalk the sidelines of many of today's varsity games, exhorting the Big Red to victory.

In reality, a bear—and a real, live, bear at that—made its first appearance on the Cornell sporting scene fifty years after the University's founding. Over the next quarter century, bears were only sporadic visitors on campus. These bears, who

The author and the 1973 bear (Bill Quain '74) at Schoellkopf Field. Collection of the author.

were flesh and blood, honey-loving, mischievous, and, at times, ill-tempered, gave Cornellians the tradition of the Big Red Bear—the much-loved, unofficial mascot of our alma mater.

Much has been said about these founding bears, but as is typical with oral histories, particularly on a college campus where stories are recast every year, the bears' history has become muddled. It is time that the true tale of these bears is recorded so that their tradition—our tradition—is based on facts (as we know them).

Touchdown I – 1915.
Cornell University Department of Athletics
and Physical Education Archives.

CHAPTER

1

THE FIRST BEAR

Cornell began playing football in 1869, but it wasn't until 1915 that the Big Red had its first undefeated season. In fact, the 1915 season is in the record books as one of the greatest ever. Cornell was declared the number one team in the East (then the center of college football) by Walter Camp and Grantland Rice, the leading football commentators of the time.

This was the age before national polls, and consequently there were usually disagreements about which team was Number One. Some sports writers contended that Pitt, which had also gone undefeated in 1915, and even Harvard, which had gone thirty-three games without a loss before falling to Cornell that season, were more worthy champions. The latter choice, however, was dismissed by E. A. Batchelor, sports writer for the *Detroit Free Press*:

> I must confess that I have been highly amused by some of the 'expert' arguments advanced in an attempt to prove Cornell isn't the eastern champion. I had been harboring the delusion that if a team beat all of its opponents decisively, including the one that was by unanimous consent hailed as the only other championship contender, there could be no dispute about the title. It seems, however, that in order to be champion you must beat Harvard some other day than the one on which you play her. This as you must concede is a hard thing to do. Championships can be won and lost only in the Yale-Harvard game and, as Cornell doesn't play in this all important event, she seems to be up against it. I would suggest that Cornell try to have it made a three-cornered affair and then if she beats both the Crimson and the Blue on the same afternoon, they will consider her claims. Personally, I believe she could have done it this season.[a]

The important story of 1915, however, is not the pundits, but the undeniable and indisputable success of the Big Red team and the on-field exploits of its stars, Charley Barrett '16 and Murray Shelton '16. Both Barrett and Shelton were named by Walter Camp to his All-American team and later inducted into the National Football Foundation's College Football Hall of Fame.

Gridiron talent aside, some of the magic of the 1915 season was conjured up by a newcomer to the Big Red football program—a black bear that was acquired by the Cornell University Athletic Association (CUAA) "as a mascot for the Varsity eleven"[b] with "money the squad raised by subscription."[c] *The Ithaca Journal* announced the arrival of the bear in a brief notice on September 25, 1915:

> For the first time in Cornell's athletic history the football team is to have a really truly live vivacious bear as a mascot. The cub was bought by Manager Hunkin and Assistant Manager Lalley at Old Town, Maine and will be named 'Gib' in honor of Gib Cool, the varsity center.[d]

The *Cornell Daily Sun* first reported this additional member of the football team on September 30, 1915, stating that the bear was acclimating to his new environs prior to his first appearance "in an official capacity."[e] This debut would be at the second game of the season, a home contest against Oberlin on October 2nd. The *Sun* also indicated that the bear had not yet been named, but that among the possibilities, "'Touchdown' will doubtless receive consideration." (One wonders whether Gib Cool had an aversion to bears.)

Before we go on with our story, one question must be asked. Why did the Big Red football team want a bear, or any other animal for that matter, as a mascot, given that the team had experienced success without one for a number of years? The answer may lie in the fact that "in the early decades of the 20th century, as revenues from ticket sales became a valuable source of revenue, intercollegiate football took on many attributes of the entertainment world."[f] The CUAA depended on ticket sales for its funding and was under pressure to promote interest in football games. Numerous *Sun* articles from fall 1915 talk about the obligation of students to support Big Red teams by buying tickets through subscriptions to the CUAA. (The *Sun* asked rhetorically in an op-ed piece that appeared on October 2, 1915: "Do you know that Cornell maintains its athletic teams on less than one-third the income received by other Universities such as Yale, Harvard, and Princeton?"[g]) Perhaps someone in the CUAA thought having a novelty such as a bear cub at the games would increase attendance and help narrow the gap between the Big Red and the "Big Three."

The real answer, however, is not so strategic or pre-meditated. As related by S.E. "Booty" Hunkin '16, manager of the 1915 football team (and from whom we have personal recollections about the first bear), "Back in the summer of 1915, I received a letter from an animal trainer in Maine asking if we would have an interest in a black cub bear for a mascot at $25.00 [nearly $500 today] plus shipping charges".[h] Booty replied in the affirmative, presumably after consulting his funders, and the cub arrived on campus in late September.

Looking back, one can only imagine how things might have turned out if the animal trainer had offered up another type of animal. Fast forwarding to 1942, the Cornell Zoology Department proposed that a pet opossum named Emory be named the University symbol instead of a bear.[i] The name "Emory" notwithstanding, it is fortunate for future generations of Cornellians that the offer was either rebuffed or ignored, given the opossum's habit of playing dead.

There was, however, historical precedent for a bear on the Hill. In 1872, Burt Green Wilder, professor of zoology, kept a bear in the basement of McGraw Hall and took the animal on frequent outings onto the Arts Quad. This bear participated in a number of pranks, including a surprise visit to the University chaplain, before falling victim to Professor Wilder's dissecting tool.[j]

But we digress. Returning to the fall of 1915, the Big Red football team beat Oberlin handily. The *Cornell Alumni News* reported, without elaborating, that a bear "was tethered on the field"[k] during the game. In a letter that was reprinted in the Sun several days later, the writer asked, "Has the bear been named yet? If not, I would like to suggest 'Victory Bruin' [brewing] or 'Vic' for short."[l]

Perhaps because he lacked a name, the bear kept a low profile over the next several weeks. According to Booty Hunkin, the bear was lodged in the Bacon Baseball Cage (on the site of what is now Hoy Field) and was an "expensive pet and, regardless of the nursery song, this bear did not like porridge. He lived on comb honey and even at wholesale from the College of Agriculture, he required a wholesome allocation of funds."[m]

The other reason why the bear was not the center of attention was that the brand new Schoellkopf Field was being prepared for its dedication on Saturday, October 9, 1915, prior to the game against Williams College. (Before the construction of Schoellkopf, the team used Percy Field, the present site of Ithaca High School.) After many long dedicatory speeches that Saturday afternoon, the Big Red improved its record to 3 and 0 by making quick work of the Williams "Ephs."

From the Cornell University Department of Athletics and Physical Education Archives.

Touchdown I – 1915.
Cornell University Department of Athletics
and Physical Education Archives.

TOUCHDOWN HITS THE ROAD

The 1915 Big Red football team continued its winning ways the following week with a lopsided victory in the "Battle of the 'nells," beating mascotless Bucknell. (Bucknell would not become the Bisons for another six years.) By this time the bear had become a fixture at Schoellkopf:

The black bear cub which the football squad bought in Maine for a mascot has been named Touchdown. The cub is a playful little beast and the crowd finds him amusing in the intermissions of football games. He is tethered on the field and has a high stepladder to climb up on. His quarters are in the training house.[a]

The next game on the schedule for the 4 and 0 Big Red was Harvard, which was riding high with a thirty-three game winning streak. The *Sun* reported that the team was scheduled to leave Ithaca for Cambridge on Thursday night to "meet the Crimson in Season's First Stiff Game," and would be accompanied by the bear. "A cage has been secured for 'Touchdown,' the bear mascot, and it makes its first appearance on foreign ground Saturday."[b] With a name and a pending road trip, things were indeed looking up for Touchdown the bear.

The Boston headquarters for the Cornell contingent, including Touchdown, was the Lenox Hotel. As Booty Hunkin recalls, "Mr. Pryor, then manager of the Lenox, guaranteed complete room service and strained honey if we would leave the cage overnight in the lobby."[c] It is unknown whether this offer was made because bears were not welcome upstairs at the Lenox or because Mr. Pryor, like the CUAA, thought a bear cub, if seen by visitors, would improve sales. More likely, Mr. Pryor (whom I suspect was not a Cornell Hotelie) was in cahoots with Harvard. This theory is based on the fact that when Booty Hunkin and his assistant, Walt Lalley '17, awoke Saturday morning after a long night consisting of dinner at

the Lenox Hotel and a smoker at the nearby Hotel
Victoria, they found the cage empty. As reported in
the *Cornell Alumni News*:

> At the dark hour of four on Saturday morning
> several young men walked into the hotel and
> told the clerk they had come to take Touchdown
> out for his morning constitutional. The clerk,
> thinking the men were 'Cornells' and suspecting
> no evil, offered no objection. They turned out
> to be some of 'the Harvards.' Manager Booty
> Hunkin and Assistant Manager Walt Lally [sic]
> were horror-stricken when they heard of the kid-
> napping. The team was demoralized. Search was
> of no avail. The first clew [sic] came from Frank
> Sheehan [Cornell's trainer]. Frank had gone out
> to Soldiers Field [Harvard's football stadium] to
> get the team's quarters ready. He telephoned that
> he had heard Touchdown crying in the neigh-
> borhood of the stadium and had traced the cub's
> sobs to the baseball cage. The managers assem-
> bled a posse which included Sport Ward '11 and
> several other loyal alumni and motored to the
> field. The janitor there was obstinate. He would
> not unlock the cage without orders from the
> Harvard football manager. He offered to admit
> the posse to his office so they might telephone
> to the manager. After he had unlocked the office
> door and before he had repocketed his bunch
> of keys he was thrust into the office and locked
> in by the determined Cornellians. The rest was
> easy, for the posse had the keys.[d]

The bear was sprung and, as chronicled by Booty, returned to the Lenox via taxi, seated "beside the cab driver and was back in the act of climbing the goal post by game time." This climbing activity was, according to Booty, the bear's habit: "His specialty was climbing the goal posts before every game. I believe it was almost an omen of good fortune when he opened up each game with spirit and enthusiasm in showing off before the spectators."[e]

Whether it was the pre-game heroics of the posse, Touchdown's aerial display, or the fact that "Cornell was just enough stronger, just enough better, and just enough more finished,"[f] the Big Red defeated the Crimson 10-0. This marked the first time Cornell had ever bested Harvard at football, and the Big Red established itself as the team to beat in the East.

The Big Red team wasn't the only talk of the town; Touchdown was becoming a star in his own right. In the custom of the day, away football games would be telegraphed back to Ithaca and a play-by-play of the game would be announced in Bailey Hall to students who paid twenty-five cents for a ticket. To add to the spirit of these gatherings, entertainment was also provided. For the "broadcast" of the Harvard game, the *Sun* announced that "the Cadet Band will give a concert starting at 2:30 p.m. and will also play between the quarters. Lantern slides of the various members of the Cornell and Harvard teams as well as pictures of the football coaches and 'Touchdown' the bear mascot will be shown between plays."[g] The cheers of the Bailey faithful must have been heard all the way to Cambridge that Saturday.

Virginia Tech was next on the schedule, and the Big Red dispatched the Hokies handily, running its record to 6 and 0. Grantland Rice was sufficiently impressed to write in his *New York Tribune* sports column:

> Cornell's place at the athletic top is now unchallenged. With records she has made upon the track, the water, the diamond and the gridiron—taking the general average—there is none to compete... Cornell to-day is in the front of the intercollegiate parade. She is Number One as far as the general average of all sport goes. And Number Two isn't very close on her heels.[h]

The Big Red now readied itself for a road trip to Ann Arbor to face off against the Michigan Wolverines. (You can imagine the disappointment of Touchdown when he found there was no opposing mascot; although Michigan adopted the wolverine as its mascot in 1861, an actual animal was never in residence until 1927.)[i]

Prior to the Michigan game, Touchdown was the guest of the Statler Hotel in Detroit.[j] It was at Detroit's Tuller Hotel, however, where Touchdown made his mark. Booty Hunkin recollects that during a pre-game dinner at the Tuller, the bear "ran amuck in the dining room and created havoc with the waiters and diners who scrambled out without returning to pay their dinner checks."[k] The reason for this boorish behavior might be that Touchdown, prior to his entering the dining room, had been riding the hotel elevator and visiting a café adjacent to the hotel.

Perhaps the aggressive pre-game play of the Cornell mascot intimidated the Wolverines, but regardless of the reason, the Big Red soundly defeated Michigan for Cornell's seventh win of the season. The reputation of Touchdown was growing, and the week after the Cornell-Michigan game, in the highest form of flattery, a Yale alumnus gave his alma mater a live mascot — an English bull dog named Brutus — ostensibly to help the Elis turn around their season.[1]

Touchdown I holds a football in its paws (the "1915," however, was added to the photograph at the time). From the Cornell University Department of Athletics and Physical Education Archives.

Touch-Downs Record.
Cornell.

13	Gettsburg._____	0
34	Oberlin._____	7
46	Williams._____	6
41	Bucknell._____	0
10	Harvard _____	0
45	Virginia _____	0
34	Michigan _____	7
40	Wash-Lee._____	21
24	Pennsylvania._____	9

Touchdown I at Franklin Field.
From 1916 Cornellian.

TOUCHDOWN TRIUMPHANT

The following Saturday, the Big Red defeated

Washington & Lee, setting up the final match

of the 1915 season against archrival University of

Pennsylvania on Thanksgiving Day at Franklin

Field in Philadelphia. As was customary, the

football team set off mid-week for Atlantic

City to "prepare" for the big game. Of course,

Touchdown was on the traveling squad and

settled in with the team in the fashionable Haddon Hotel on Atlantic City's fabled boardwalk.

Touchdown, however, did not appear to be overly impressed with America's Playground. According to Booty Hunkin, Touchdown "had followed the instincts of his parents and had gone to sleep for the winter," resting in the baggage room of the hotel. Touchdown was a celebrity, though, and the Philadelphia press demanded an audience. As Booty remembers, "against my advice, Lalley dragged the little fellow on his belly to the porte-cochere of the hotel and, after considerable prodding, got him on his feet" to pose for the cameras.[a]

That's when things got interesting. Touchdown, obviously annoyed that his nap had been disturbed, broke loose and ran up the ramp to the boardwalk, chased by Booty Hunkin and Walt Lalley. The bear ducked into the first open store, which happened to be a taffy shop, and chased two taffy pullers who came out "wild eyed."[b] Instead of stopping to sample the wares, Touchdown ran down to the beach into the ocean—undoubtedly another first for the cub from the woods of Maine. As Booty tells the story, "we had to get a life boat from under the board walk and with no oars and hand paddling we finally got him ashore."[c] The bear then walked back to the hotel on his own, no doubt both exhilarated and enervated from the day's activities.

RIVAL MASCOTS

The team finished its pre-game preparations and traveled to Philadelphia. This was to be Touchdown's first and only visit to Franklin Field. Again in Booty's words; "When we brought him out on Franklin Field that Thanksgiving Day, he was only half conscious and it was questionable if he would even climb the posts. However from across the field came the Penn cheerleaders with a coyote. Just as the bear touched noses with the coyote, he fired a right cross to the head and the coyote rolled over and over."[d] The *Cornell Alumni News* described the Penn mascot that day as a "wolf dog of the 'husky' type."[e] Coyote or husky, notwithstanding, its tryout as mascot was a failure thanks to Touchdown.

Touchdown (with Booty Hunkin and Walt Lalley) and the Penn 'Coyote' at Franklin Field. From 1916 *Cornellian.*

Winner by a knockout, Touchdown "was led out to one of the goals, {where} he clambered part way up one of the uprights, but refused to climb as high as the cross-bar despite continued urging. His failure to make the distance was greeted with a shout from the Pennsylvania stands and was evidently regarded as a bad omen for Cornell."[f] The two teams played even for the first three-quarters of the game before Cornell put on a furious fourth quarter effort and vanquished Penn 24-9. The *Sun* proclaimed Cornell, "Unbeaten and Unbeatable!"[g]

Thus, the first undefeated season in the history of Cornell football was achieved. And one would assume that Touchdown, who stood with the Big Red since the second game of the season, would be the toast of the team and the university. And he might well have been feted as a hero if fate had not intervened. While Cornellians celebrated throughout Philadelphia that Saturday evening, the team managers took all the equipment and Touchdown, who was dead asleep in his cage, to Reading Terminal for the train trip back to Ithaca. In the station, Booty Hunkin was asked by a Cornell alumnus from Rome, New York, what the team intended to do with the bear. Booty hesitated, not knowing what would happen to Touchdown when he arrived back in Ithaca. Then Booty recalled the events of the last several weeks, and came to the realization that the bear cub asleep in the cage in front of him was destined to become a 500-pound giant with a commensurate appetite for honey and who-knows-what-else. Looking at his beaver-lined broadcloth coat that Touchdown had "ripped from collar to hem and dragged through the mud"[h] earlier that day, Booty asked the fellow from Rome what he had in mind. The alumnus said he wanted to start a zoo in Rome and thought Touchdown, as the "best known bear in America,"[i] would be just the attraction to get things going. Booty recalled, "it didn't take long to change the shipping tag and the CUAA was saved the express charges and a big board bill yet to come."[j]

There is no record of Touchdown taking up residence in Rome. On the contrary, the *Cornell Daily Sun*, ran a front page story on December 2, 1915 titled, "His Work Well Done, 'Touchdown' Leaves":

> 'Touchdown', Cornell's first real mascot, and one who was with the most remarkable football team Cornell has produced, will today be sent back to Old Town, Maine from where it came last September. The bear, it has been found would have been so large by next season, that keeping him until then would be extremely impractical. An exchange, for a smaller bear, as 'Touchdown' was in September, will be effected next fall.[k]

We don't know whether the aspiring zookeeper had second thoughts or if something else happened that caused his plans to go awry. Regardless, going back to the Maine woods was certainly preferable to a life of confinement for Touchdown. We can hope that Touchdown I (for there were to be successors) lived a long and contented life in the north woods.

Touchdown II with
G. Ervin Kent '10,
graduate manager
of athletics.
Courtesy of the
Division of Rare and
Manuscript Collections,
Cornell University Librar

TOUCHDOWN II

The 1916 Cornell football team started its season

with high hopes. Memories of the glory of 1915 were

still fresh, as were the images of a bear prowling

the sidelines. Keeping faith with the send-off

of Touchdown the prior December, Walt Lalley

'17, now manager of the football team, was given

the responsibility of recruiting the new bear.[a]

We don't know if Walt went back to the same animal trainer, but the *Cornell Alumni News* reported that "a black bear cub has been imported from Maine. His name, like that of his predecessor, is Touchdown."[b] First impressions, however, were not positive; our old friend Booty Hunkin described the new bear as "too ugly to be safe."[c]

Touchdown II kept a low profile during his first month on campus, during which the Big Red won its first three games. Harvard was the next opponent and, with a record of 4 and 1, the Crimson eleven were among the best teams in the East, along with Penn, Yale, and Cornell. Remembering the Cambridge bear heist the prior year, the *Sun* ran a front page notice titled "No Touchdown for Harvard:"

> 'Experience is the best teacher.' Touchdown I, Cornell's premier mascot spent part of his stay in Cambridge last year in enforced confinement in the cage of the Harvard Gymnasium. It was not until a few minutes before the game that his place of hibernation was discovered, and he was brought out on the sidelines. His unopposed climb up Harvard's goal post presaged Cornell's 10-0 victory.
>
> Touchdown II, who left with the team yesterday afternoon, will be under the custody of S.H. Ayer '14 [composer of "Cornell Victorious," a favorite fight song] and C.W. Schmidt '17 during his entire stay at Cambridge. He will only be let loose on Soldier's Field.[d]

Harvard, apparently intent on winning the rematch, expended no energy trying to kidnap Touchdown II and beat Cornell 23-0. Despite the loss, a mascot and a tradition were in the making. An advertisement titled "Touchdown," placed in the *Sun* by Rothschild Brothers, Ithaca's legendary and late-lamented department store, featured "clever imitations of the mascot that immediately fascinate every maid." The ad goes on to say, "this little bear is just the right size for your partner to carry to the game, and not only is a clever gift but it makes a novel way to show your colors."[e]

The Big Red football team rebounded with three straight wins over Carnegie Tech, Michigan and the Massachusetts Aggies. Touchdown II, however, stayed out of the limelight, perhaps resting up for the return trip to Atlantic City and Philadelphia.

The final game of the 1916 season, against Penn, was again played at Franklin Field on Thanksgiving Day. Penn got its revenge for the prior year's loss at the hands (and feet) of the Big Red by defeating Cornell 23-0. Cornell came out on the short end on the sidelines as well. The *Cornell Alumni News* reported, "Cornell had Touchdown II at the field, but Pennsylvania this year had a bear of their own and he was the better mascot of the two."[f]

Not only was Touchdown II bested by Penn's bear, but he was also left behind to fend for himself. As reported by the Philadelphia press, "Touchdown II, the Cornell football team's bear mascot was deserted by the Ithacans after the Penn game Thanksgiving. When the shades of night were blackening Franklin Field the little bear was boxed by 'Gibby' the caretaker at the grounds. There was no parading around for little Touchdown II as his elder friend Touchdown I of 1915 enjoyed after the Penn Game last season. Gibby gave the bear a loaf of bread and stood guard over him with a club so that no one would walk over him as Penn did to the Lake Cayuga team."[g]

If that wasn't insult enough, it was reported that Touchdown II accompanied the Penn team to Pasadena to play the Oregon Ducks in the Rose Bowl, and that his cage mate was "Jack Victory," Penn's own ursine mascot.[h] We can only hope that the cage was large and the trip was short.

We do not know the fate of Touchdown II. With luck the bear stayed in California instead of being consigned to wander the wilds of West Philadelphia.

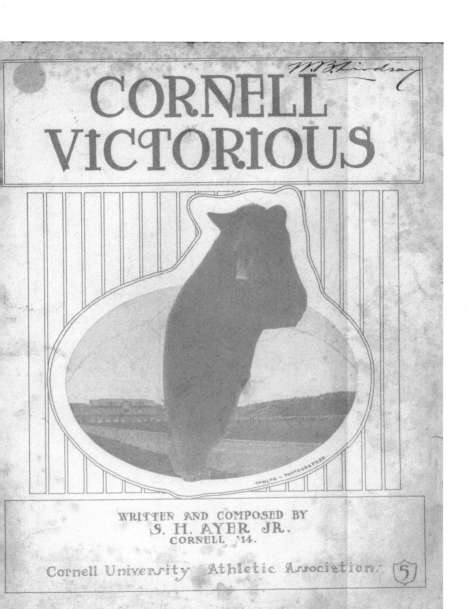

ver of sheet music for *Cornell Victorious* with Touchdown II. From the author's collection.

Touchdown III with Coach Rush and
Rym Berry '04, at Schoellkopf Field.—1919.
Collection of the University of Pennsylvania.

CHAPTER
5

TOUCHDOWN III

The 1916 season marked the end of normalcy for several years as the Great War gripped the world and Cornell. As Morris Bishop described in his *History of Cornell*, "the University, and the country [were plunged] in a bath of seriousness, doubt, questioning."[a] Certainly the minds of students on the Hill were occupied by concerns other than pet bears, and the campus went without a bear in 1917 and 1918.

The 1919 football season, the first "back to usual" campaign following World War I, saw Touchdown III, a gift of a Montana alumnus, R.H. Barney '17, on the roster. Lest anyone think that this was only of local interest, the *New York Times* reported:

> The Cornell football team is to have a real, honest-to-goodness mascot this season. It has all Ithaca 'by the ears'. A near holiday was declared when the news was wafted, as news will be, through the city that a bear cub fresh from Montana had arrived to be chaperon of the Red and White eleven on the gridiron this season. For the first time in a long while Cornell is wearing a 'Please don't feed or annoy the animal' shingle. If Ithaca wasn't dry, it probably would be drinking a bear of a toast.[b]

Touchdown III was not the toast of all in Ithaca, however. The bear "appeared on campus without an OK from the new graduate manager Romeyn Berry '04."[c] "Rym" had been appointed the head of the CUAA (the predecessor position to the present-day director of athletics) earlier that year and, as he made clear on numerous occasions, he was not a fan of the bear mascot. Rym announced, "They smell badly and their personal habits are disgusting. They are dangerous, ill-tempered and unbelievably troublesome."[d]

Rym had only limited experience with the first two Touchdowns and may have been parroting the sentiments of Booty Hunkin, who recollected,

"[Touchdown] was not cute and cuddly as it matured. It became perpetually hungry, mean, ill-bred and dangerous. When allowed to climb the goalposts it was hell trying to get him down and a menace to try and recage him."[e] It was clear, regardless of where Rym got his bear facts, that during the time he was in charge of the CUAA, bears would be a less-than-welcome presence at Cornell.

But Touchdown III was already on campus and hopes were high for the football team to return to national prominence. The *Sun* reported that "Touchdown the Third, the frolicsome cub bear, Cornell's mascot this season, is the admiration of the entire squad, as well as the coaching staff."[f] One of those coaches was W.C. "Gib" Cool '16 for whom the first bear was to be named before being given the handle, "Touchdown."

The Place to Buy 'Em is Where They Have 'Em

CORNELL ATHLETIC ASSOCIATION
FOOT BALL
SCHEDULE FOR 1919

H. M. MAC CABE, MGR.
ROMEYN BERRY, Grad. Mgr   W. T. TERRY, Asst. Mgr.
J. H. RUSH, Coach

Compliments of **THE R. W. COUCH CO.**
205 Dryden Road

If It's Spalding's We Have It

Touchdown III with H.M. MacCabe '20, manager of the 1919 football team. *Cornell Alumni News,* July 1966.

The Big Red opened the 1919 football season against Oberlin on an unseasonably hot October Saturday afternoon. The *Sun*, in its recap of the 9-0 Cornell victory, said "Touchdown the Third was also among those who did not approve of the weather, for the little cub bear, Cornell's mascot, signified his distaste by refusing (at first) to climb the goal post. Yielding to the pleadings of Manager H.M. McCabe '20, Touchdown scurried up the padded pole, perched contentedly on the cross bar for a few minutes, and then expressed his satisfaction by hurriedly descending. It was even too hot for the little bear cub."[g]

The following week, the importance of Touchdown III to the fortunes of the Cornell football team was highlighted in an article on the front page of the *Sun* titled, "Touchdown III Loses at Game of Hide and Seek:"

> The varsity football squad faced disaster for the entire season when Touchdown III disappeared from Schoellkopf Field yesterday. The little woozy cub had forsaken his haunts on Schoellkopf Field, but how, no one knew. Volunteers, compets, and freshmen were deputized in the search to recover the mascot. But sunshine again beams on the moleskin wearers, for the black beauty has been found. Quietly snoozing in the grass below Schoellkopf Field, the searchers found Touchdown. He was taken to his den, and once more tramples his chained area.[h]

The next game of the season was against Williams, and the Big Red eked out a 3-0 win. The bigger story in Ithaca that day was the inclement weather and a student demonstration for higher professors' salaries. Touchdown III joined in common cause with the demonstrators, leading a parade in front of Schoellkopf with students and the football team carrying placards reading "Feed the Profs," "A Professor Teaches on His Stomach," and "$125,000 Will Feed a Prof and His Family for a Million Years."[i]

Touchdown III demonstrating on behalf of professors. Cornell University Department of Athletics and Physical Education Archives.

Campus politics, however, were only a distraction for Touchdown III, and the bear began preparations for a trip to New York City with the team, which was to play Dartmouth at the New York Polo Grounds. The team was booked into the new Hotel Pennsylvania, but hotel management (certainly not Cornell Hotelies) made it clear that Touchdown was not welcome. Instead, according the *New York Times*, the bear had to go "directly from Pennsylvania Station to the Cornell Club, on Forty-fourth Street, where he is to be the guest of honor Friday evening at a big Cornell smoker."[j]

To be accurate, a twin bill was in store for those attending the smoker. According to the *Cornell Alumni News*, "the feature of the smoker will be stunts by Louis A. Fuertes '97 and Touchdown III."[k] But that probably was not the end of it. The *Sun* reported "Due to a cloud of mystery that surrounds the affair no program was obtained, however, Touchdown III, it is said will be the center of attraction."[l] Whatever went on that night is lost to history. Perhaps all those in attendance were pledged to observe the time-honored rule, "What goes on at camp, stays at camp."

Dartmouth beat Cornell in New York, and by the time the annual Thanksgiving Day game with Penn rolled around, the Big Red's record was a disappointing 3 and 4. Although the team headed back to Atlantic City to prepare for its game with the Penn Quakers, there is no record of the bear making the trip. With the contest against Penn of little consequence, interest in pulling out all of the stops to ensure victory was in short supply.

The Big Red took a defeat at Philadelphia and, with its season now over, Touchdown's duties were also complete. According to legend, the bear was packed off to a zoo in Akron, Ohio.

Touchdown III lives on, however, in the fight song of one of the Big Red's rivals to the south, the Nittany Lions of Penn State. Cornell and Penn State started playing each other in football in 1893 and faced off in Ithaca during the 1919 season. The Lions beat the Big Red 20-0 and, while no formal record

exists of Touchdown attending the game, he must
have made an appearance. We deduce this from the
fact that some time after the game Jimmy Leyden,
Penn State '14, wrote the "The Nittany Lion Song,"[m]
an homage to the Penn State mascot, which
mentions the Cornell bear:

> *There's old Pittsburgh with its Panther, and Penn her Red and Blue,*
> *Dartmouth with its Indian, and Yale her Bulldog, too.*
> *There's old Princeton with its Tiger, and Cornell with its Bear,*
> *But speaking now of victory, we'll get the Lion's share.*

When the Cornell–Penn State rivalry picked up again
in 1936, it was the Bear who got its share.

Touchdown III with H.M. MacCabe '20, Coach Rush, and Rym Berry '04, at Schoellkopf Field.
Collection of the University of Pennsylvania.

Touchdown III and Rym Berry,
Cornell University Department of Athletics
and Physical Education Archives.

CHAPTER

6

THE BEAR-LESS YEARS

Given Rym Berry's feelings about bears, it is not

surprising there was no successor to Touchdown III

during the rest of Berry's tenure as head of CUAA,

which lasted until 1935. This period coincided with

that of the Big Red's legendary football coach, Gil

Dobie. "Gloomy" Gil coached from 1920 to 1935

and won more games than any coach in Cornell

history. His taciturn personality was reflected in his

approach to the game: "hold'em, fight'em, and beat'em, and don't depend on anything but brawn and determination."[a] Mascots of any sort had no place in Dobie's game plan, and the Cornell bear became a distant memory.

By the fall of 1934, Rym Berry was being eased out of his position due to CUAA's deteriorating financial position and Dobie's teams were facing declining fortunes. Coincidentally (or not), a movement to bring back the bear began to stir.

It all started with a dance. According to the custom of the day, a "hop," with big-time entertainment, was held before most home football games. As reported in the Sun, "the eagerly awaited announcement of the motif of the decorations for the Dartmouth Hop on Friday night has at last been released by the committee. In keeping with the major athletic event of the weekend, the decorations themes will be the Dartmouth Indian and the Cornell Bear."[b] In the same issue of the Sun, a less-than-enlightened advertisement for the Hop was placed titled, "The Indian and The Bear":

> Friday evening will find wild life running rampant through the drill hall when the Cornell bruin and the Dartmouth Redskin meet in a pre-game encounter. Get the bare facts about the Indian's chief worry at the Dartmouth Hop. Watch Bruin brave the Brave—There'll be plenty trouble brewin'!! Be there when the Bear bares the brave Brave's weaknesses. Tickets now on sale.[c]

The pre-Hop hype continued in the *Sun* with articles titled "Cornell Bear Rises from Past to Claim Share of Spotlight"[d] and "Cornell Bear Returns to Scene of Triumphs for Dartmouth Hop"[e] that featured somewhat hazy and embellished stories about Touchdown I. Touchdown II and III obviously had faded into obscurity.

The *Cornell Alumni News* reported that "apparently the bear and the Indian [in the form of life-sized paintings] were happy mascots for the party in the Drill Hall [now known as Barton Hall], where students, fraternity house guests and some more staid members of the community, it is said, danced to the seductive strains of two orchestras far into the night."[f]

The next day Cornell beat Dartmouth on the football field and the "return" of the Cornell Bear was credited with the win. With Penn next up on the schedule, interest in the bear heightened; if a life-sized painting of the Cornell Bear could help the Big Red, certainly a real bear would be decisive in besting the Penn Quakers.

The Sun reported the Monday before the game that the "rally committee announced 'Touchdown' the original Cornell bear mascot would attend the celebration and was already on his way to Ithaca from his wilderness haunt."[g] Touchdown I would have been nineteen years old at this point, certainly getting on in years, but probably still spry enough to make a curtain call in support of his team.

The night of the Penn Rally, an overflow crowd gathered at Bailey Hall to cheer on the Big Red team and to meet Touchdown. Unfortunately, no bear appeared. In Touchdown's absence, the bear-detractor himself, Rym Berry, "obligingly served as a last minute substitute for Touchdown 'IV' dressed in a fur coat."[h] Rym may have been a bad judge of bears, but he lived up to his reputation for good humor and panache.

There is a story behind the story, however. The rally organizers had every intention of delivering a live bear to Bailey for the event. According to the *Cornell Alumni News*, "three {Cornell} undergraduates arrived at Burnett Park {Zoo} in Syracuse {the day of the rally} with a home-made cage on a trailer and succeeded in persuading the keeper that they had permission to borrow a bear. The bear, however, thought otherwise, and bid fair to demolish the cage before he could be returned safely to his own lair in the zoo."[i]

The morning after the rally, a columnist for the *Sun* opined:

> If Cornell is going to use the Bruin as its official emblem, we should at least adopt it whole-heartedly. Should the student body favor its adoption at the close of this season, perhaps the honorary societies, or some fraternity on the Hill, or even an alumnus, might be persuaded to present a bear cub to Cornell; and it could be

kept here permanently and displayed at pep rallies, et cetera. Young Bruin might even have a special keeper, chosen by competition, and make the trips with the team. If he brings us luck in the Penn game as he did in Dartmouth, we're all for the Bruin.[j]

Neither a bear nor Lady Luck showed up at Franklin Field in Philadelphia in November 1934, and the Quakers defeated the Big Red (despite what Grantland Rice described as one of the "gamest" efforts he had ever witnessed).[k]

In a seeming effort to put a stake in the heart of what might have remained of the bear movement, Rym Berry wrote an article in the *Ithaca Journal* several weeks after the Penn game:

> There are signs that the students of Cornell again want a bear as a mascot. This is ominous, because what the students want they are apt eventually to get. And there are broken men at Schoellkopf who might still be young and vigorous, poetical, trusting, and alert but for their previous, disillusioning experiences with bears.

> Students like bear mascots—for about a week. They buy them collars, decorate their quarters, bring them food from restaurants, and try to teach them tricks. And then their interest wholly reverts to cultural studies and warm gin.[l]

Rym then took the offensive: "...with all these wolverines, panthers, tigers, bull-dogs, mules, goats, bears, mustangs, badgers, and buckeyes now in the business, Cornell would seem to enjoy a unique and dignified distinction in having no mascot at all."[m]

Realizing that this logic was not likely to win over the student body, he then went on to suggest that if "students insist and must have some pet to love them and bite them and smell the place up, why not select something which shall be at once distinctive, original, imaginative and practical? How about a goldfish or a parrot?"[n]

Two years later some further ursine-stirrings must have prompted Rym, no longer head of athletics, but the author of a column in the *Cornell Alumni News* to write:

> Contrary to the first report widely distributed by the papers, this year's {1936} football team will not have a bear mascot. Faculty children are sorry about this, but employees of the Athletic Association, who have known bear mascots and to the extent are acquainted with grief, are hysterical with joy. The last bear mascot, Touchdown IV, occurred in 1919. The fetid odor of the disagreeable beast still lingers in the baseball cage where he was kept.[o]

With this article, Rym firmly established himself as a wet blanket on the topic of bears, and proved himself unable to count. The appearance of Touchdown IV was still three years in the future.

Touchdown IV
at the Press Clubhouse
in Forest Home.
Collection of Robert Sto

CHAPTER

7

RETURN OF THE BEAR

The official 1938 Big Red Football program featured a bear carrying a football, but it wasn't until 1939 that another real bear prowled the Hill. Much had changed at Cornell in the twenty years since Touchdown III. Morris Bishop described this period at the university as "one of material progress—the endowment nearly doubled, the value of the buildings, grounds, and

equipment nearly trebled."[a] New buildings, including
Baker Laboratory (1923), Willard Straight Hall (1925),
Balch Hall (1929), the Gothics on West Campus
(1931), Myron Taylor Hall (1932) and Martha Van
Rensselaer Hall (1933), were now campus landmarks.

Cornell athletics also had entered a new era. The
Rym Berry-Gil Dobie years were over, replaced by
Jim Lynah '05 as athletic director and Carl Snavely
as football coach. Lynah took over Rym Berry's job
in 1935 and became the first director of the new-
ly-formed Department of Physical Education and
Athletics. He was a businessman who had a mandate
to put Cornell athletics on firm financial footing.
Snavely came from the University of North Carolina
where "his record was excellent, his standards high,
and his personality genial."[b] His job was to return
Cornell to gridiron glory, and he did it well. The
1939 football season would go down in history, along
with the 1915 season, as one of the most successful
and momentous in Cornell annals.

The extraordinary achievements of the 1939 football
team were almost eclipsed, however, by bear number
four. Touchdown IV was to leave her mark on that
memorable fall and her story is particularly well-
documented in the *Cornell Daily Sun*. The *Sun*
editorial board, if not directly responsible for
Touchdown IV, was a co-conspirator with the Press
Club, the social journalistic society that brought
the bear to campus.

The story begins with six members of the Press Club
in the fall of 1939. Five lived at 310 Forest Home

25c

ENN STATE vs CORNELL

TICIAL PROGRAM   OCTOBER 22, 1938

III No. 2

Drive in what they referred to as the Press Clubhouse. According to one of the residents, "a lot of brilliant plans were hatched there, one of which was the Cornell football team ought to have a live bear mascot."[c] Bill Page '40, a member of the Press Club, was elected to implement the plan. Bill recollects that he purchased Touchdown IV, a six-month old female black bear (females supposedly being less aggressive than males), "from a Nashua, New Hampshire animal farm in mid-August '39 for $50 [nearly $700 today] including a shipping crate. I [Bill] brought Touchdown to Forest Home and my first stop in Ithaca was a local insurance agent where I bought for $100 a Lloyds of London liability policy."[d] Given the relative costs of Touchdown I and Touchdown IV, a bull market in bears had flourished in the intervening twenty-four years.

The Press Club, which had adopted the bear as its mascot, hoped that the 1939 football team would do the same. Bob Storandt '40, editor-in-chief of the *Sun* and a Press Club member, remembers that the only problem was "a chap by the name of Jim Lynah who seemed to have even more clout than we [the *Sun* editorial board and the Press Club] did, and Lynah thought having another bear mascot was a lousy idea."[e]

Lynah's dislike of bear mascots may have reflected his no-nonsense approach or the residual influence of his predecessor's low opinion of bears. Either way, the director of athletics was on a collision course with the *Sun*.

The first public notice of Touchdown IV's presence on campus appeared on October 5th in a page one story in the *Sun* titled "Big Red Footballers May Have Mascot":

> Unconfirmed rumors to the effect that Cornell's football team might have a bear cub as a mascot came to a climax yesterday when a small Canadian Black Bear made its appearance on the campus. Renewing a not-forgotten tradition of the Cornell Bears, Touchdown will be the fourth bear cub mascot the Big Red gridders have had. Although the present animal is quite tame and already well trained, all necessary precautions reported taken to protect both the cub and onlookers. A specially constructed cage, insurance and special diet are among these precautions.[f]

On the op-ed page in the same issue, the *Sun* editors (Bob Storandt and others) reported that the bear had:

> ...looked over Ithaca and Cornell while being transported to his local quarters. A little skeptical at first, he soon gave it all his Official Bear OK. That in brief is the story so far: Bear OK's Cornell. What he's wondering about, however, is whether Cornell will OK him. But don't be mistaken, Touchdown isn't the least bit modest and he's sure Cornell will think he's the tops. What he is a little concerned about though is an official OK from the Athletic Association. Now

Touchdown isn't a great big ferocious grizzly bear. He's just a little fellow and all he asks is a chance to help. Fact is, here we've been calling Touchdown a "he" all the way through. But Touchdown is really one of the gentlest of gentle females. Touchdown has already made scores of friends. They've promised to take the best care of him. And when football season is over, they guarantee his safe return to New Hampshire from whence he came. You know why now this is no ordinary bear. So of course he's insured. That will cover all damaged or eaten Orange gridmen {of Syracuse}, and the rest. He has promised to put in an appearance at each of the home football games. Moreover, his friends have planned for his attendance at several away games. So now you know about Touchdown IV. He's ready and waiting to do his part for Cornell 1939 football. He's ever so happy here and wants to stay. And he hasn't a worry in the world. Except—as we said before—an official OK from the Athletic Association. The AA's directors will be visited this morning and asked for their official sanction. Please, good sirs, mayn't we keep our Touchdown?[g]

It is not known who made the overture to the Athletics Department, but Jim Lynah refused permission for the bear to appear at any football games.[h] This led to the first of many salvos fired in (and by) the *Sun* to appeal the decision. An open letter in the *Sun* from Touchdown IV to Lynah read:

Dear Mr. Lynah,

I am a black bear. I am just a little black bear. I'm a Canadian cub.
At least that's what it said in the *Sun* yesterday so I'm told; but of
course I can't read, so I wouldn't say for sure. Anyway, a while ago some
Cornell fellows invited me to come down here for the football season.
They said they thought I'd be good to arouse "spirit", whatever that
is. Now I didn't come right away on account I'd heard about the three
other bears who had been here in past years, and who, I guess didn't
make out so well. But I came and here I am. Now I'm told that you
won't let me stay. But why, please, sir? I have a reputation of being one
of the best-behaved bears alive, next to maybe Winnie the Pooh and
nobody's quite sure that he's alive. Don't you think I don't realize that
your University has to take care of its students, faculty members, players,
customers, and everybody at football games. But honest I wouldn't hurt
any of them. Why I'll even wear thick leather boots on all four paws
and a wire muzzle. Then surely sir I couldn't hurt anybody.
Really I'll wear all these precautions and I won't mind. I'm insured too,
you know. All covered on liability—why I don't know, because I surely
don't mean to hurt anybody. I'm sure I would be able to build up the
spirit stuff too. And I plenty understand the team is going to need
plenty of it when it plays Syracuse tomorrow afternoon. I wouldn't want
to hang around for the whole game either. Why I could just come in
between the halves. I could have two leashes with a good strong man
on the end of each and my muzzle and leather boots. Then you see,
I'd be so safe that I couldn't possible hurt any one. I'm ever so playful
Mr. Lynah. Just look at my picture and see how cute I am when I stand
up and cross my paws. Do I really look big and ferocious? Please let me
come on the field, just for a little while between the halves. I can help
Cornell and I do want to. Aw gee, I was afraid you wouldn't like me.
But please, Mr. Lynah, won't you reconsider. I know Cornell wants me
and I'm very so enthusiastic about Cornell.

Respectfully yours,
Touchdown IV [i]

Lynah was unmoved and "issued a final ultimatum that there were to be no bears admitted to the field, or adjoining grounds."[j] But there was equal resolve on the other side. The *Sun* reported that:

> ...an undisclosed, but authoritative source told the *Sun* last evening Touchdown will 'definitely appear on Schoellkopf Field this afternoon during the Cornell-Syracuse game'. The *Sun's* informant did not indicate how the bear's sponsors planned to penetrate the 'bear scouts' which the Athletics Department is expected to post at every entrance to Schoellkopf Field, 'But you can tell Cornell that we mean to have a bear there during the football game and nobody's going to stop us'."[k]

As she prepared for her debut, Touchdown IV settled into life in Forest Home and became a local attraction. The *Sun*, in a regular column called "Berry Patch," described the bear as

> ...a lovable little creature who stands about three feet high and fits into a rather small sized doghouse where he now reposes, both literally and figuratively. Our first acquaintance with him was the shine of a wet nose through the doorway of his house, a nose that sniffed forward to our hand, exploring, questioningly, and then contentedly. His ears are soft and well furred and his eyes are shoe button black and quite large for a bear of his size. He sits on his haunches

with his paws folded over his very comfortable paunch and gazes at you for all the world like a fat German butcher sunning himself in front of the store. "Darling" was the girlfriend's opinion when she saw him with the little leather boxing gloves that have been made to enclose his diminutive paws. She didn't care so much for the muzzle that he wore around his head. We judged it unnecessary too, but it is true Touchdown couldn't bite a peanut while he has it on.[l]

This description apparently didn't tell the whole story. Bob Storandt remembers that he sported a bandage on his hand in the early days of that fall semester as a result of Touchdown's affections.[m]

Touchdown IV
at the Press Clubhouse
in Forest Home.
Collection of
Robert Storandt.

Touchdown IV at the Straight rally.
Bob Storandt '40 is the driver and
Bill Page '40 is the keeper.
Collection of Robert Storandt.

THE BATTLE OF THE BEAR

Despite the promises of the bear's promoters,

Touchdown IV did not make an appearance at the

Syracuse game. Her assistance apparently was not

required, as the Big Red started its 1939 season

with a 19-6 victory. Off the gridiron, the battle

lines were drawn; members of the Press Club

sensed an opportunity to turn a light-hearted prank

into a way to needle the humorless Jim Lynah.

Although the bear was "officially" unwelcome at Schoellkopf Field, Sigma Delta Chi (the professional journalistic society with mutual membership with the Press Club) decided that a rally in front of Willard Straight Hall, Cornell's student union, was just the thing to galvanize public support for the bear cub and change the mind of the athletic director. The *Sun* editors wrote, "Our estimable Mr. Lynah knows better than best and what is important. He has made up his mind that the bear is not the thing for this campus. And that is very definitely that. Or is it? Only you [the student body] can answer."[a]

The rally went off as planned, but according to the *Sun*, the bear "spent most of the time in a tree. Escorted by members of Sigma Delta Chi the small black bear performed for the five hundred Cornellians gathered in front of Willard Straight Hall at noon before she started her sojourn amid the leafy tops. Once entrenched on a limb about 20 feet above the ground, the bear refused to budge. Her keepers pleaded, Touchdown held on tighter. Finally, an emergency call to the Straight brought forth a ladder and Bill Page affected a 'heroic' rescue. Petitions advocating the bear's acceptance by the CUAA [the Athletics Department] were circulated."[b]

Touchdown IV at the Straight rally. Collection of Robert Storandt.

Unwilling to let the facts speak for themselves, the *Sun* editors "reported:"

> "Bear, Bear, Bear" This is a story about a little bear cub who went to the Cornell campus yesterday noon, took a good look around, climbed a tree and generally sold herself to all who met her. She was still a "dangerous" bear, but still wore no muzzle or leather boots, which she has among her belongings. And there are no dead today, as a result. No clawed arms. No bear-bit Cornellians limping around the Hill.

Touchdown IV with admirers at the Straight rally. Cornell University Department of Athletics and Physical Education Archives.

It was all a little new to Touchdown, So, somewhat upset, she scrambled up a tree. Or maybe she wanted to get where everyone could see her better. Then she glanced wonderingly over to Schoellkopf Field, home of the CUAA. Apparently no one from there was coming over to see her; apparently no one from there cared much what she looked like. Then she scurried back into her private car and was driven home where she probably is now playing in the sun, or gnawing contentedly on a carrot or piece of apple. She wants Cornell to know how much she appreciates all the petitions signed in her favor. Touchdown likes Cornell and wants to stay. Cornell obviously like Touchdown and wants her to stay. Will she be able to stay? To come to the games? That depends. No matter how much we want Touchdown to stay, no matter how much needed we feel she is, no matter how many petitions are filled, no matter how playful and friendly she is—on the last analysis, whether or not she will stay depends on something more. Depends on one man [Jim Lynah] who can send forth one word from Schoellkopf Field.[c]

Princeton at Princeton was the second football game of the season, and in response to an inquiry, the Princeton Athletic Office agreed that Touchdown could attend the game, but only if Cornell officials gave their approval. Princeton went so far as to feature Cornell's would-be-mascot on the cover of its official game day program.

This triggered the next appeal that took the form of an editorial in the *Sun* titled "The AA {Athletics Association} and More Bear:"

There has been an unquestionable and substantial improvement in the management of Cornell physical education and athletics in recent years under the generally capable direction of James A. Lynah. The {Athletics} Association's immense debt has been encouragingly reduced. New branches of athletics have come under its wing. A highly worthwhile intramurals program has been widened. Numerous steps have been taken to expand and improve the facilities of the AA. James Lynah has done some splendid work and we do not in any sense seek to tear down his accomplishments. But occasionally the AA has erred; occasionally it has lost sight of student interests for which it must consistently have a definite concern; occasionally therefore, the *Sun* has criticized its tactics. We feel that the current question of admitting a small bear cub to home football games is one which the AA is in positive error. Admittedly the experience of the Schoellkopf directors with past bear mascots has been unfortunate. Sometimes they have been dangerous; always they have been a bother to the AA. But is that reason to set up an arbitrary "No" to all future bears? We think not. The hundreds of signatures on petitions before us assure us that we are not alone in so thinking. Take the two outstanding elements of objection: Danger and Bother. The bear has proved already that she is scarcely dangerous. With the proper

muzzling and foot-padding of Touchdown, the objection becomes ridiculous. As for bother, the bear is being cared for entirely under private supervision. She would at no time be a burden to the AA. A letter has just come from the Princeton athletic office. It reads "...this association has no objection, proving you accept all the responsibility in the matter." That from Princeton. Nothing from Cornell. But Touchdown's sponsors ask nothing more from Cornell. We concede too, that in his original refusals Mr. Lynah was justified in making his decision. Since then, however, sufficient evidence has certainly been advanced to invalidate any reasonable objection. Touchdown is wanted, safe and no bother. It is still not too late for a reversal of what at present stands as purely arbitrary and unreasonable 'No'.[d]

The *Sun's* conciliatory approach proved unsuccessful. No approval of Touchdown IV was forthcoming from Jim Lynah, who had decided the bear was too "dangerous."[e] On the day of the Princeton game, the *Sun* reported, "Touchdown, might-have-been mascot of the Big Red gridiron forces, sat mournfully on the front lawn of her Cornell home this morning and speculated on the outcome of today's game. The football team had gone to Princeton, but not Touchdown. So today the tiny Canadian bear cub will spend despondently nibbling apples, and wondering what a football game is like."[f]

The Big Red handily beat the Princeton Tigers
and returned to Ithaca to get ready for the Nittany
Lions of Penn State. The official program for the
Penn State game previewed the contest as a battle
of beasts:

> Again the Nittany Lion roars and heads north.
> Nittany is the name of the mountain range that
> surrounds the peaceful vale where Penn State stu-
> dents nestle down for an all too brief four years'
> surcease from the tribulations of a battle-scarred
> world. The Mountain comes to Cornell this time
> loaded for bear. Mixing up our metaphors still
> further, we see the Lion leading a powerful safari
> into the Cayuga Reservation in an attempt to
> tame Cornell's mascot, which the powers-that-be
> have banned from the ball park. Is Touchdown
> IV banned because he may get hurt by the
> ferocious Lion? Or is Touchdown IV too tough
> for the Nittany wildcat. We know the Lion has
> tasted blood, and that spells bad business for all
> who come in its path. Without the aid of our
> black bear Carl Snavely [Cornell's coach] will
> throw eleven tried and trusted warriors against
> the invader. The outcome? Your guess is as
> good as ours.[8]

The Big Red, still without Touchdown on the side-
line, chased the Nittany Lions back to Happy Valley
in a 47-0 rout.

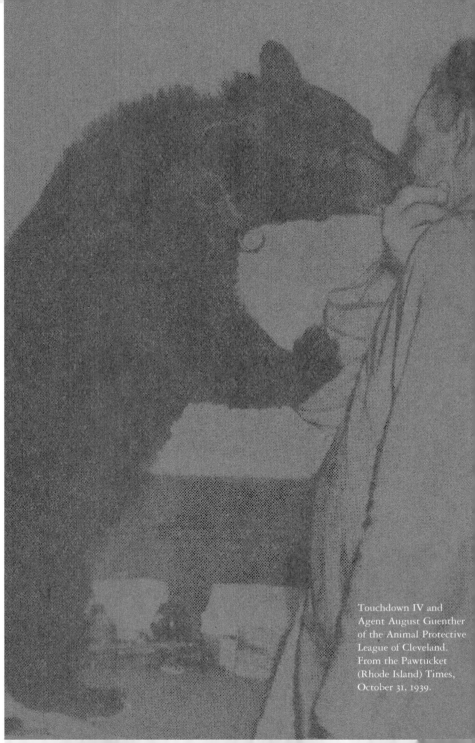

Touchdown IV and
Agent August Guenther
of the Animal Protective
League of Cleveland.
From the Pawtucket
(Rhode Island) Times,
October 31, 1939.

TOUCHDOWN AND THE BUCKEYES

By late October of 1939 Touchdown and her

supporters were becoming increasingly impatient

with the Athletics Department. With the most

important game a week away—a face-off against the

undefeated Ohio State Buckeyes, leaders of the

Big Ten—the *Sun* ran another and more pointed

piece, imploring Lynah to recognize the bear:

We also note though not with as much

pleasure, that Touchdown IV, Cornell mascot,

trying-to-be, was not present on the field [at the Penn State game]. Mister Lynah seems to have forgotten about the little bear too easily. Mister Lynah made his first decision against the little bear without ever having seen the little animal. Now he knows about it and is still stubbornly refusing to give the little gal an audience. Is Mister Lynah counting on the usual Cornell apathy to tide him over objections from various parts of campus. We don't understand Mister Lynah's stubbornness in refusing to reconsider his decision. It seems a bit childish. The bear is small and friendly, equipped with leather gloves to sheath its diminutive claws, a muzzle and a strong leather collar to which are attached a pair of steel chains; also Touchdown is fully insured and has her board and lodging paid for by a private source. Yet Mister Lynah talks of danger and responsibility. One must realize Mister Lynah is a very busy man (in common with all big business executives) and has very little time to spend thinking about the likes and dislikes of the student body. Football is big business at Cornell as well as it is elsewhere, but so long as the corporation is going to bear the name of Cornell, should not the incumbent student body have a small interest in the affairs of the business? We don't think that this asking too much. But since the Athletic Association is a business corporation it is interested in making money. Money depends on attendance at the games — attendance depends on school interest and school spirit. We think that the recognizance of Touchdown IV would pay dividends in school spirit. Dividends! — Mister Lynah — The successful businessman should recognize them when he sees them.[a]

This appeal was met with a deaf ear, but things were about to change. A fateful chain of events was to unfold that was completely out of the control of Lynah and, ultimately, Touchdown's admirers and caretakers. J. Bently Forker '26, president of the Cornell Club of Cleveland, sent a letter to the *Cornell Daily Sun* (which was printed in the *Sun* on October 24), inviting Touchdown to the Ohio State game in Columbus. Bently Forker writes, "We will reserve free space on the Cornell-Ohio State Football [railroad] Special leaving Cleveland Terminal at 9:30 a.m. next Saturday. Touchdown IV will attend the Baggage Car Ball, be wined and dined and attend all other festivities as an honored guest of the Cornell Club of Cleveland."[b]

As it turns out, Bently Forker was put up to extending the invitation by one of the directors of the Cornell Club, James Webb '09, whose daughter was dating none other than Bill Page '40 who had brought Touchdown to campus several months earlier.[c] Bently may have had ulterior motives, but he was in common cause with the pro-bear campaign being waged on campus. He writes, "We sympathize with the problems of Touchdown IV. It is just impossible to keep a bear in the doghouse for very long. We realize also that it is no fun to go to football games, and leave a bear behind." Bently then signs off, "We like bears."[d]

CORNELL CLUB OF CLEVELAND

DON'T JUST GET EDUCATED—KEEP EDUCATED

SEASON 1939-40

October 21, 1939

To the Editor of the Cornell Daily Sun
Ithaca, N. Y.

We sympathize with the problem of Touchdown IV. It is just impossible to keep a bear in the doghouse for very long. We realize also that it is no fun to go to football games, and leave a bear behind.

One solution would be to use the bear for the official mascot this season, with the agreement that at the end of the season, the bear be disposed of at a zoo. It also might be presented then to my friend, Hank Bowdish '26, who is now manager of Bear Mountain Inn. Hank always wanted a bear. He told me so, when he was a freshman. He ought to have a bear for local color.

At any rate, we will reserve free space on the Cornell-Ohio State Football Special, leaving Cleveland Terminal at 9:30 A.M. next Saturday, for Touchdown IV and one guardian. All other guardians $3.50 round trip. Touchdown IV will attend the Baggage Car Ball, be wined and dined, and attend all other festivities as an honored guest of the Cornell Club of Cleveland. We like bears.

Yours very truly,

J Bently Forker

J. Bently Forker '26
President
Cornell Club of Cleveland.

Letter from the collection of Robert Storandt.

The *Sun* editors quickly accepted the invitation on behalf of Touchdown IV in an open letter to the Cornell Club of Cleveland:

We also like bears. Because we do, we appreciate the interest evidenced by the Cornell Club of Cleveland in the problems of Touchdown. But as you already know, we have tried repeatedly and without success to convince Mr. Lynah that Touchdown should be accepted as official mascot of the Big Red football team. Mr. Lynah's refusal leaves our hands tied. We cannot therefore assume the responsibility of bringing the bear cub to the Ohio State game ourselves, without any sort of official sanction from the Cornell Athletic Association. Touchdown has graciously received your generous invitation, but it only increases her dilemma. She has an extremely attractive offer, but no apparent means of accepting it. We will, however, be delighted to ship the bear — Prepaid Express — to the Cornell Club of Cleveland immediately. She could then go to the game as your guest, and after the party you have only to ship her back to Ithaca to us. We are sorry that Mr. Lynah's stand on bears is in opposition to that of so influential an alumni group as the Cornell Club of Cleveland. We sincerely hope you will find it possible to accept our offer and regret that the action of the Athletic Association prevents further cooperation. We are glad you like bears.

*The Cornell Daily Sun*ᵉ

In a return telegram to the *Sun*, Mr. Forker indicated that Henry Taylor of the Ohio State Athletic Association had approved the bear attending the game; Ohio State has had "goats, geese, lion cubs, wildcats, turkeys, wolves and a snake in the stadium" and is not "afraid of a bear."[f] That settled, all that remained between Touchdown and Columbus was a 300 mile train trip.

We can assume that Touchdown IV had an uneventful journey from Ithaca to Cleveland, which was the stopover before Columbus. In fact, she looks rested and relaxed in a pre-game picture taken by the {Cleveland} *Plain Dealer* that shows her draped with a Cornell pennant and posing with Bently Forker and "Red" Zeman '15, of the Cornell Club of Cleveland.[g] We also can assume that the Cornell Club was good to its word and Touchdown IV enjoyed VIP treatment on the Cornell-Ohio State Football Special that left Cleveland for Columbus on game day.

The *Plain Dealer* reported that although the intent was for Touchdown IV to patrol the sidelines, "for some reason or other [she] was locked up under the Ohio State stadium and never appeared on the field."[h] Even if Touchdown had created any excitement at the game, however, she would have been overshadowed by one of the epic moments in Cornell football history.

Given little hope of matching up with the reigning Big Ten champion, the Big Red defeated Ohio State in a come-from-behind thriller. The *Plain Dealer* reported, almost lyrically, on page one, "From far above Cayuga's waters, a big Red avalanche today crashed down upon Ohio State's national football title aspirations. Up from nowhere, from two touchdowns behind in a never-to-be-forgotten rally seldom eclipsed for brilliance and bravery, a great Cornell team demolished the Buckeye battalion, 23-14."[i]

THE CORNELL DAILY SUN

TOUCHDOWN IV AT OHIO STATE

(Courtesy of the Cleveland Plain Dealer).
Touchdown IV is shown before the Ohio State game with Ladimir (Red) Zeman '15, left, and J. Bentley Forker '29, vicepresident and president, respectively, of the Cornell University Club of Cleveland.

Cornell Daily Sun,
October 30, 1939.

In the definitive history of Cornell athletics, the book *Good Sports*, Bob Kane, who was Jim Lynah's assistant in 1939, recollects, "It was a wild scene on the Cornell side, even to the point where ordinarily composed, rational people went bananas. Athletic Director Jim Lynah nudged me rather energetically and exclaimed, 'For three years I've been a dumb [expletive deleted] and today I suppose I'm a smart guy.'"[j] Maybe Lynah was referring to the fact that he had, at long last, not vetoed Touchdown's attendance at a game.

One can only imagine the celebration that wound back to Cleveland that night. Touchdown was right in the middle of it and, in fact, became the story. An Associated Press piece that ran nationally on the Monday after the game, titled "Touchdown IV in Cleveland Jail" reported:

> Climbing nightclub potted palms landed Cornell University's would-be bear cub mascot in the clink here [Cleveland] tonight. Master Touchdown IV was a model of mascot conduct at the Cornell-Ohio State football game at Columbus on Saturday. Afterward, he was put on a special train enroute to Cleveland. It seems that some Cornell sympathizers, high spirited over their victory, enticed Touchdown off the train and into a more or less snooty Cleveland entertainment resort. Anyway, there he was ogling the pretty chorines, eating popcorn and well on his way up the trunk of a potted palm when agents of the Animal Protective League were summoned. The League locked him

up and declined to discuss the matter. It appeared
that Touchdown's keeper sold him to a Cleveland
alumni [sic] who inadvertently sold him to two
other parties. They are now looking for the owner.[k]

Versions of this story ran in hundreds of newspapers
big and small across the country, with headlines pro-
claiming "Cornell's Cub Cuts Up at Night Club,"[l]
"Bear Cub, Cornell's Mascot, Has Gay Time With
Cleveland Night Clubbers,"[m] and "Touchdown IV,
Cornell Mascot Captured."[n]

On that Monday, the *Plain Dealer* ran the back story
titled "Cornell Cub in Custody After Night Club Spree":

GRIDIRON OSCULATION FOR AND BY A TOUCHDOWN

Kissing and touchdowns went hand in paw yesterday.
At the left, George Marshall, owner of the Washington
Redskins, kisses his wife in celebration of a touchdown
scored by his team against the Packers. On the right

Touchdown IV, Cornell bear cub mascot who got into
trouble while sampling Cleveland's night life, enjoys his
confinement at the Animal Protective league by mugging
with Warden A. H. Guenther. **(A.P. WIREPHOTO)**

On the train coming back to Cleveland Saturday night everyone was happy, what with Cornell winning 23-14, etc., etc. It had been ascertained that Bill Page would sell Touchdown for $25. A collection was taken up and the bear became the joint property of Cleveland alumni. The alumni then appointed a 'bear committee' to decide what to do with Touchdown. The committee went into conference and decided the bear should be sold. Part of the committee went one way and part another, offering the mascot for sale to everyone in the train.

On arrival in Cleveland the committee met again and discovered it had sold the bear twice, once to John Russell [Cornell '29] of Franklin, Pa., and once to Carl Moellman of Gates Mills [Ohio]. One committeeman deftly solved that situation by tearing up Moellman's check.

Then, as a suitable climax to the whole affair, [Bently] Forker could not find the bear when the train pulled in. Forker went to the Hermit Club where some alumni were going. No bear. He went to Shaker Tavern. No bear there, either. About midnight somebody phoned him that the bear was having a fine time in the Hotel Cleveland 'Bronze Room'.

It seems that Gordon Stofer [Cornell '36] had charge of the bear most of the time at the hotel, but he disclaims responsibility for subsequent events. 'Somebody put a rope in my hand and I looked around and there was a bear', he explains.

Anyway there were about a dozen from the train who wandered into the Bronze Room. Touchdown was a big hit there, just as it was everywhere. Especially with the women. At every table the women petted the bear and fed it pop corn. 'This is the life', thought Touchdown. 'I'll just hibernate through my hangover.'

At one time the bear slipped its chain and was running loose around the lobby, much to everyone's consternation. Bellhops and alumni pursued it around chairs and tables and finally captured it trying to climb a potted palm.

Somebody — no one knows who — called the Animal Protective League. Agent August Guenther took Touchdown into custody. But the bear was still in full spirits and resented being caged. At league headquarters it climbed a post and got out, and it was some little time before Touchdown decided to call it a night.

Since 3:00 a.m. yesterday [Sunday], the league headquarters has been deluged with calls from alumni wanting Touchdown released. Henry L. Leffingwell, superintendent of the league, left orders that the bear was not to be released until this morning [Monday] when he gets to his office.

His aides at the league headquarters say that he is under the impression that the bear had been tormented and that schools ought not use animals as mascots and he is going to tell 'em so before the bear is given up. Besides all that, the league wants some proof of ownership by somebody.

[John] Russell went back to Franklin, Pa. yesterday without the bear. He said he was going to present Touchdown to the Pennsylvania Conservation Commission. Forker said he would get the bear today and ship it to Russell by express.°

Front page,
October 29, 1939.
©1939 *The Plain Dealer*.
All rights reserved.
Used with permission of
The Plain Dealer.

On Monday, Superintendent Leffingwell decided to take John Russell up on his offer. The bear would be released from custody and shipped to Russell in Franklin "to be turned loose in the mountains to return to his primitive state."[p]

"From the Ivy League to the Animal Protective League and now to the Pennsylvania woods" is how James Doyle, a columnist for the *Plain Dealer*, summed up Touchdown IV's journey. Doyle elaborated:

> Touchdown IV was en route to the tall timbers in his big red crate as these lines were written, a gift to the Pennsylvania State Game Commission, and today he'll be far from the maddening throng. Growling, perhaps, that they can have their football clubs and their night clubs, but give him the hills and the trees and the babbling brooks.
>
> 'It's a good break for everybody else as well as for Touchdown, himself' observed Mr. Red Zeman yesterday, 'that he is going to spend the rest of his life in the forest. It hasn't been in the papers, and I wouldn't want it to go any further, that on the way back from Columbus he took a hearty bite out of President Bently Forker of our Cornell Club of Cleveland, and a bit of a bite out of me, the vice president. He got Forker in the leg and me in the arm. But I'm wondering if somebody on that train hadn't fed him something in way of spirits.'[q]

To show that he did not nurse any sore feelings, Bently Forker raised a toast to Touchdown at a Cornell Club of Cleveland luncheon held at Fischer-Rohr's, a legendary downtown Cleveland restaurant, several weeks after the excitement:

> There is no connection between Touchdown IV and the Bear steak dinner served by Fischer-Rohr's. Reports from Pennsylvania are that Touchdown is having the time of her life. Her French-Canadian accent has taken the little Pennsylvania Dutch bears by storm, and has given her no mean social standing. After all, she is the only bear that ever visited the Bronze Room and had sumptuous quarters at the University Club.[r]

Touchdown was not around to see the end of what is arguably Cornell's finest football season. The Big Red team went on to win the rest of its games to finish 8 and 0, and was ranked fourth in the country behind Texas A&M, Tennessee and the University of Southern California. Looking back on the season, Jim Lynah could take small comfort that the team's fortunes were not inextricably linked with the bear he would not allow to be the Big Red's mascot.

The *Cornell Daily Sun* bid farewell to Touchdown IV in an editorial titled "Queen for a Day:"

Little did Touchdown realize what was in store for her when she was brought down from the cold Northern wilds to act as mascot for the Big Red football team. Despite a poor reception on the part of the Cornell Athletic Association, Touchdown still managed to be queen — if only for a day. She reigned supreme when the Cornell Team made history out in Ohio. Coming back from Columbus with wildly jubilant alumni, Touchdown behaved courteously but when she reached Cleveland she could no longer contain herself and off she went to paint the town a Carnelian red. She ended up in a dog cage in the custody of the Animal Protective League. Today Touchdown realizes the error of her ways. Ousted from her throne, Touchdown is on her way back to the wilds. We hope she hasn't forgotten her bear lore while she has been in Ithaca. Perhaps she was pampered too much with sweet foods. Perhaps she was protected too much. We sincerely hope Touchdown manages to get along and make a comfortable living. Goodbye Touchdown and Good Luck![s]

The Athlete in
front of the Straight.
Photo by Robert Barker.
Collection of the author.

The Scholar in
front of the Straight.
Photo by Robert Barker.
Collection of the author.

And that's the end of the story of Touchdown IV and the three other real bears who once roamed the Hill. Although there would be no Touchdown V, we hold dear the four bears who called Ithaca home in 1915, 1916, 1919, and 1939, making an indelible mark on Cornell.

These bears certainly were of a different era, when fans traveled by train to cheer on their gridiron heroes, the Big Red competed for national football championships, and young women were called chorines.

Despite all that has changed, much remains the same at Cornell. Students still demonstrate on campus, pull pranks, and engage in lively discourse with the university administration. And the legacy of Touchdown lives on; students in bear suits cavort on the sidelines, and there is even a budding movement among the student body to bring back the bear (but this time in bronze).

There are physical reminders on campus of the bears. The architectural firm of Delano and Aldrich which designed Willard Straight Hall in 1921 included a "characteristic Cornell animal"[a] in the

The Memorial Room bears. Photos by Robert Barker. Collection of the author.

decorative flourishes. Two carved wood bears stand sentry at the back of the Memorial Room, and two stone bears (shown on the inside covers of this book) flank the fireplace in the International Lounge. Just inside the main entrance of the Straight, over the vestibule door, another bear peeks over the Cornell emblem. And in clear view of any person who walks by the Straight are two carved stone bears on each side of the main entrance. One of these bears is bespectacled and reading a book, and the other is clutching a football—the scholar and the athlete.

In September 1915—the one hundredth anniversary of the first bear's arrival on campus—a bronze statue was dedicated to the memory and tradition of the four Touchdowns. It is placed in front of Teagle Hall and casts a look toward Schoellkopf Field where Touchdown I witnessed Cornell's first national championship football team. The effort to erect this statue was led by Joe Thanhauser '71 and John Foote '74 and was supported by the gifts of several hundred alumni and friends, all of whom thought it was high time Touchdown returned home.

The influence of the four Touchdowns is both pervasive and permanent in their imprint on the "Cornell character"[b] (borrowing Carl Becker's phrase). Perhaps Morris Bishop had these bears in mind when he wrote about the "the spirits who have dwelt upon this hill in the century past":

Past lives, past thoughts and emotions,
are not utterly lost; they linger faintly
in our own thoughts, our own emotions.
There are old ghosts about us.
They reappear in dreams and sudden recollections;
they help to make us all Cornellians;
they are the spirit of Cornell.ᶜ

—Morris Bishop

	WON		LOST	

9-0 | 1915 season

SEPTEMBER 28	**13** Cornell	**0** Gettysburg	at Ithaca
OCTOBER 2	**34** Cornell	**7** Oberlin	at Ithaca
OCTOBER 9	**46** Cornell	**6** Williams	at Ithaca
OCTOBER 16	**41** Cornell	**0** Bucknell	at Ithaca
OCTOBER 23	**10** Cornell	**0** Harvard	at Cambridge
OCTOBER 30	**45** Cornell	**0** V.P.I.	at Ithaca
NOVEMBER 6	**34** Cornell	**7** Michigan	at Ann Arbor
NOVEMBER 13	**40** Cornell	**21** Washington & Lee	at Ithaca
NOVEMBER 25	**24** Cornell	**9** Pennsylvania	at Philadelphia

	WON		LOST	

6-2 | 1916 season

OCTOBER 9	**26** Cornell	**0** Gettysburg	at Ithaca
OCTOBER 14	**42** Cornell	**0** Williams	at Ithaca
OCTOBER 21	**19** Cornell	**0** Bucknell	at Ithaca
OCTOBER 28	**23** Harvard	**0** Cornell	at Cambridge
NOVEMBER 4	**15** Cornell	**7** Carnegie Tech	at Ithaca
NOVEMBER 11	**23** Cornell	**20** Michigan	at Ithaca
NOVEMBER 18	**37** Cornell	**0** Mass Aggies	at Ithaca
NOVEMBER 30	**23** Pennsylvania	**0** Cornell	at Philadelphia

	WON	LOST	

3-5 | 1919 season

OCTOBER 4	9 Cornell	0 Oberlin	at Ithaca
OCTOBER 11	3 Cornell	0 Williams	at Ithaca
OCTOBER 18	21 Colgate	0 Cornell	at Ithaca
OCTOBER 25	9 Dartmouth	0 Cornell	at NY Polo Grounds
NOVEMBER 1	21 Lafayette	2 Cornell	at Ithaca
NOVEMBER 8	20 Cornell	0 Carnegie Tech	at Ithaca
NOVEMBER 15	20 Penn State	0 Cornell	at Ithaca
NOVEMBER 27	24 Pennsylvania	0 Cornell	at Philadelphia

	WON	LOST	

8-0 | 1939 season

OCTOBER 7	19 Cornell	6 Syracuse	at Ithaca
OCTOBER 14	20 Cornell	7 Princeton	at Princeton
OCTOBER 21	47 Cornell	0 Penn State	at Ithaca
OCTOBER 28	23 Cornell	14 Ohio State	at Columbus
NOVEMBER 4	13 Cornell	7 Columbia	at Ithaca
NOVEMBER 11	14 Cornell	12 Colgate	at Ithaca
NOVEMBER 18	35 Cornell	6 Dartmouth	at Hanover
NOVEMBER 25	26 Cornell	0 Pennsylvania	at Philadelphia

Notes

CHAPTER 1

[a] *Cornell Daily Sun*, December 7, 1915, p. 5.

[b] *Cornell Daily Sun*, September 30, 1915, p. 1.

[c] *Cornell Alumni News*, October 7, 1915, p. 13.

[d] *Ithaca Journal*, September 25, 1915.

[e] *Cornell Daily Sun*, September 30, 1915, p. 1.

[f] University of Pennsylvania online archives.

[g] *Cornell Daily Sun*, October 2, 1915, p. 4.

[h] S.E. Hunkin, letter to the editor of the *Cornell Alumni News*, January, 1966, p. 28.

[i] *Cornell Daily Sun*, April 15, 1942.

[j] Burt Green Wilder, "Tale of the Cornell Bear on the Cornell University Campus", *The Cornell Review*, Vol. II No. 2, November 1883,

[k] *Cornell Alumni News*, October 7, 1915.

[l] *Cornell Daily Sun*, October 5, 1915, p. 4.

[m] S.E. Hunkin, letter to the editor of the *Cornell Alumni News*, January, 1966, p. 28.

CHAPTER 2

[a] *Cornell Alumni News*, October 21, 1915, p. 49.

[b] *Cornell Daily Sun*, October 21, 1915, p. 1.

[c] S.E. Hunkin, letter to the editor of the *Cornell Alumni News*, January, 1966, p. 28.

[d] *Cornell Alumni News*, October 29, 1915.

[e] S.E. Hunkin, letter to the editor of the *Cornell Alumni News*, January, 1966, p. 28.

[f] *Cornell Daily Sun*, October 25, 1915.

[g] *Cornell Daily Sun*, October 23, 1915, p. 1.

[h] *Cornell Alumni News*, November 4, 1915, p. 11.

[i] www.umich.edu.

[j] *Cornell Daily Sun*, November 6, 1915, p. 4.

[k] S.E. Hunkin, letter to the editor of the *Cornell Alumni News*, January, 1966, p. 28.

[l] *Cornell Daily Sun*, November 12, 1915, p. 4.

CHAPTER 3

[a] S.E. Hunkin, letter to the editor of the *Cornell Alumni News*, January, 1966, p. 28.

[b] ibid.

[c] S.E. Hunkin, letter to Charles C. Colman Class of 1912 president, July 7, 1976.

[d] S.E. Hunkin, letter to the editor of the *Cornell Alumni News*, January, 1966, p. 28.

[e] *Cornell Alumni News*, December 2, 1915.

[f] ibid.

[g] *Cornell Daily Sun*, November 26, 1915, p. 4.

[h] S.E. Hunkin, letter to the editor of the *Cornell Alumni News*, January, 1966, p. 28.

[i] *Cornell Alumni News*, December 2, 1915.

[j] S.E. Hunkin, letter to the editor of the *Cornell Alumni News*, January, 1966, p. 28.

[k] *Cornell Daily Sun*, December 2, 1915, p. 1.

CHAPTER 4

[a] *Cornell Alumni News*, November 1983, p. 17.

[b] *Cornell Alumni News*, October 5, 1916, p. 8.

[c] S.E. Hunkin, letter to the editor of the *Cornell Alumni News*, January, 1966, p. 28.

[d] *Cornell Daily Sun*, October 27, 1916, p. 1.

[e] *Cornell Daily Sun*, November 9, 1916.

[f] *Cornell Alumni News*, December 17, 1916, p. 113.

[g] *Cornell Daily Sun*, December 2, 1916, p. 1 (Special to the *Cornell Daily Sun*).

[h] *Cornell Daily Sun*, December 2, 1916, p. 1.

CHAPTER 5

[a] Morris Bishop, *History of Cornell* (Ithaca, New York: Cornell University Press, 1962), p. 433.

[b] *New York Times*, September 4, 1919, p. 23.

[c] Bob Kane, *Good Sports* (Ithaca, New York: Cornell University, 1992), p. 48.

[d] *Cornell Alumni News*, December 6, 1934.

[e] Bob Kane, *Good Sports* (Ithaca, New York: Cornell University, 1992), p. 47.

[f] *Cornell Daily Sun*, September 29, 1919, p. 5.

[g] *Cornell Daily Sun*, October 6, 1919, p 1.

[h] *Cornell Daily Sun*, October 9, 1919, p. 1.

[i] Morris Bishop, *History of Cornell* (Ithaca, New York: Cornell University Press, 1962), p 438.

[j] *New York Times*, October 22, 1919, p. 14.

[k] *Cornell Alumni News*, October 9, 1919, p. 32.

[l] *Cornell Daily Sun*, October 24, 1919.

[m] Eberly Family Special Collections Library, Penn State University.

CHAPTER 6

[a] *Washington Post*, November 9, 1921, p. 16.

[b] *Cornell Daily Sun*, November 13, 1934, p. 1.

[c] ibid.

[d] *Cornell Daily Sun*, November 14, 1934, p. 1.

[e] *Cornell Daily Sun*, November 15, 1934, p. 1.

[f] *Cornell Alumni News*, November 22, 1934, p. 8.

[g] *Cornell Daily Sun*, November 26, 1934, p. 1.

[h] *Cornell Daily Sun*, November 27, 1934, p. 1.

[i] *Cornell Alumni News*, December 6, 1934, p. 7.

[j] *Cornell Daily Sun*, November 28, 1934.

[k] *Cornell Alumni News*, December 13, 1934, p. 3.

[l] *Cornell Alumni News*, December 6, 1934 (reprinted from the the Ithaca Journal).

[m] ibid.

[n] ibid.

[o] *Cornell Alumni News*, September 24, 1936, p. 9.

CHAPTER 7

[a] Morris Bishop, *History of Cornell* (Ithaca, New York: Cornell University Press, 1962), p 467.

[b] ibid, p 507.

[c] Bob Storandt, interview with John Foote, March 12, 2007.

[d] Bill Page, letter to John Foote, October 13, 2004.

[e] Bob Storandt, interview with John Foote, March 12, 2007.

[f] *Cornell Daily Sun*, October 5, 1939, p. 1.

[g] ibid, p. 4.

[h] *Cornell Daily Sun*, October 6, 1939, p. 1.

[i] ibid.

[j] *Cornell Daily Sun*, October 7, 1939, p. 1.

[k] ibid.

[l] *Cornell Daily Sun*, October 9, 1939, p. 4.

[m] Bob Storandt, interview with John Foote, March 11, 2005.

CHAPTER 8

[a] *Cornell Daily Sun*, October 9, 1939, p. 4.

[b] *Cornell Daily Sun*, October 11, 1939, p. 1.

[c] ibid, p. 4.

[d] *Cornell Daily Sun*, October 12, 1939, p. 4.

[e] *Cornell Daily Sun*, October 14, 1939, p.14.

[f] ibid, p. 1.

[g] "Welcome Nittany Lions!", Official Souvenir Football Program, October 29, 1939.

CHAPTER 9

[a] *Cornell Daily Sun*, October 23, 1939, p. 4.

[b] J. Bently Forker, letter to editor of the *Cornell Daily Sun*, October 21, 1939.

[c] *Cleveland Plain Dealer*, October 30, 1939, p. 1.

[d] J. Bently Forker, letter to editor of the *Cornell Daily Sun*, October 21, 1939.

[e] *Cornell Daily Sun*, October 24, 1939, p. 4.

[f] *Cornell Daily Sun*, October 25, 1939, p. 1.

[g] *Cornell Daily Sun*, October 30, 1939, p. 3 (photograph courtesy of the *Cleveland Plain Dealer*).

[h] *Cleveland Plain Dealer*, October 30, 1939, p. 1.

[i] ibid.

[j] Bob Kane, *Good Sports* (Ithaca, New York: Cornell University, 1992), p. 40.

[k] *Washington Post*, October 30, 1939, p. 17.

[l] *Cleveland Plain Dealer*, October 30, 1939.

[m] *Coshocton* (Ohio) *Tribune*, October 30, 1939.

[n] *Minneapolis Star*, October 30, 1939.

[o] *Cleveland Plain Dealer*, October 30, 1939, p. 1.

[p] *Hagerstown* (Maryland) *Mail*, October 31, 1939.

[q] James. E. Doyle, The Sport Trail, *Cleveland Plain Dealer*, October 31, 1939.

[r] *Cornell Alumni News*, November 23, 1939, p.121.

[s] *Cornell Daily Sun*, October 31, 1939, p. 4.

EPILOGUE

[a] *Cornell Alumni News*, November 22, 1934, p. 8.

[b] Carl L. Becker, "The Cornell Tradition: Freedom and Responsibility," *Cornell University: Founders and the Founding* (Ithaca, New York: Cornell University Press, 1943), p. 193.

[c] Morris Bishop, *History of Cornell* (Ithaca, New York: Cornell University Press, 1962), p. 616.

Acknowledgments

For a simple book, I find myself indebted to a lot of people.
Although I take full responsibility, the contributions of
the groups and people below are evident on every page.

Cornell Library's Division of Rare and Manuscript Collections
and the Cornell Sports Information Office were very
helpful in pulling notes and pictures out of their archives.
I am particularly grateful to Ellie Harkness and Marlene
Crockford for their interest and willingness to help.

I owe a huge debt of gratitude to Bill Page '40 and
Bob Storandt '40 who provided me with oral histories
of Touchdown IV. I treasure the afternoons spent in
Bob's living room looking at scrapbooks and listening
to his stories. I hope this book is a fitting tribute to
Bob's enthusiasm, love and respect for Cornell.

My father-in-law, Jack Rupert '49, was one of the first
people I pulled into this project. Jack, who has earned the
appellation 'Mr. Cornell', helped dispel some of the myths
surrounding the fourth Touchdown. Only Jack would be
willing spend time in the *Cleveland Plain Dealer* morgue
digging up facts—and have fun doing it.

Several people waded through early drafts and provided
knowledgeable, thoughtful and candid comments:
Tom Keating (despite being a Williams man),
Will Versfelt '07, and Larry Lowenstein '43 (a diehard
Big Red fan and one of my heroes).

Dr. Gary Gray, a Penn State gridiron legend, was very helpful in solving a mystery about the Nittany Lion Song which features the Cornell Bear. After reading a draft of this book, Gary is relieved he played in the modern era.

Toward the end of this project I was fortunate to meet the Brothers Earle: Evan '02 works as University Archivist, and Corey '07 is, as described by the Cornell Chronicle, an "apostle of Cornell History." These two gentlemen directed me to new sources of information, checked facts, polished the manuscript, and moved the project forward with their enthusiasm.

I found writing this book was only half the battle; getting it into a form to be published is an equal challenge. Karen Salsgiver Coveney '76 and Peter Coveney have been instrumental in putting this book into the end zone with great style.

Special thanks are due to my patient and supportive wife and best friend, Kristen Rupert '74, who wonders to this day how she ever married a cheerleader.

And finally, a salute to Cornell. Paraphrasing Cavafy's great poem, *Ithaca*, Cornell has given me a beautiful voyage; without her I would never have taken the road. As a small repayment, the proceeds of the sale of this book will go to Far Above…The Campaign for Cornell.

John Foote '74
Forest Home, New York, *2008*

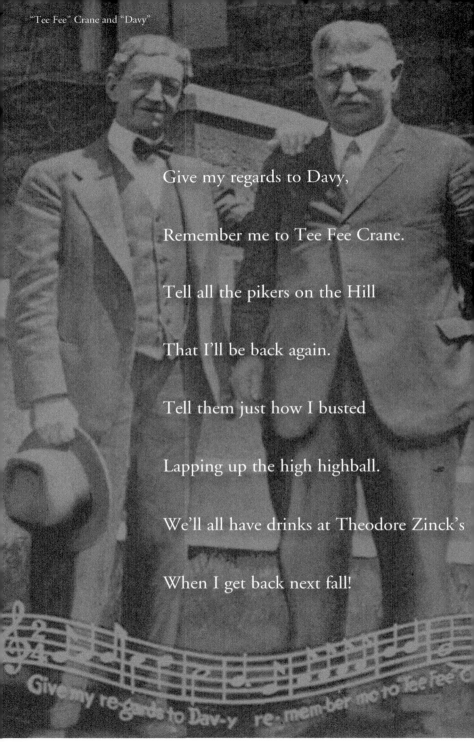

"Tee Fee" Crane and "Davy"

Give my regards to Davy,

Remember me to Tee Fee Crane.

Tell all the pikers on the Hill

That I'll be back again.

Tell them just how I busted

Lapping up the high highball.

We'll all have drinks at Theodore Zinck's

When I get back next fall!

Give my re-gards to Dav-y re-mem-ber me to Tee fee c

GIVE MY REGARDS TO DAVY

Our fight song's lyrics were written in 1905
by Charles E. Tourison '05, W. L. Umstad '06,
and Bill Forbes '06, a trio of roommates
at Beta Theta Pi, and set to the tune of George
M. Cohan's "Give My Regards to Broadway."
The song refers to a fictional encounter among
an anonymous freshman ("piker") and David
Fletcher "Davy" Hoy, Class of 1891 (for whom
Hoy Field is named), the registrar and secretary
for the committee on student conduct, and
Thomas Frederick "Tee Fee" Crane, professor
of languages and the first dean of the College of
Arts and Sciences. This encounter was provoked by
the freshman allegedly drinking a bit too much.*
David Hoy was known for his ferocity as a strict
disciplinarian. Professor Crane, on the other hand,
was generally well liked among students.**

* Songs of Cornell, complied and edited by Thomas A. Sokol;
Cornell University Glee Club, Ithaca, New York, 1988

** "Dear Uncle Ezra." Cornell University. Retrieved 2008-02-21

This book is set in the typefaces Garamond 3
and Franklin Gothic, two of the over 200 typefaces
designed by Morris Fuller Benton (1872-1948),
a prolific type designer who left his mark on
20th century design after graduating from Cornell
in 1896 with a degree in engineering. Benton
designed Franklin Gothic, an excellent all-round
display face, from 1903–1912. His Garamond 3,
a text serif font based on the punches of Jean Jannon
(1580–1635), was designed in 1917, in between the
years of Touchdown II and Touchdown III. These and
dozens of Benton's other fonts are still in use today.

A first edition of 2000 copies was printed by Finlay
Printing, Bloomfield, Connecticut, in April 2008.

The second edition, bound with soft cover,
was published by Cornell University Press in 2017.

The book was designed as a gift to Cornell by
Karen Salsgiver Coveney '76, whose daughter
Nina Coveney '11, was one of the modern-day
Cornell Big Red Bears.

The 2007–08 bear.
The Coveney family collection.